1

So before we start, I just want to clarify few things. You may have read a lot of "self help" books from these successful rich men and women. Some say in their books that you need to do so and so when in reality most of them have no idea what a lot of people in the world have to go through. Or what it's like coming from a disadvantage background. That being said this is not an attack on all the self help book authors out there, just asking you humbly not to put me on any boats as anyone else.

I am my own man, I make my own decisions and I make my own choices. I take responsibility for my actions and my actions alone. I have my own boat, I am the captain of that ship and I journey alone. I am a man that has grew up through a dark childhood, torture, poverty, inequality and injustice. Till this day I haven't tasted the richness of this world that everyone is so crazy about. I am no expert, I am just a man that is after his freedom and freedom for his people.

You may now continue to reading about my take on hustle and the grind. Enjoy!

Breathing to Hustle (Part 1)

*I'm watching everyone around me
reaching success,
Wondering when will it be my turn to get
mine,
Had enough of waiting around,
So at 14 I went out to get what's mine,*

*I have been ruthless, lawless ever since,
Powerful and unstoppable ever since,
Got my heart broken but no fear no fear,
Because the only thing breaking here is the
atmosphere,
I had my fair share of rejections,
Let me break down the game in sections,
I know setbacks so sit back and watch me
come back,*

*I can read people so don't act suspicious,
That's why she be saying I'm perspicacious,
Marry a queen and eat food that are
delicious,
Big dreams, big rooms, I like things that
are spacious,*

A new style was born from the ups and

downs,
This knowledge gave my voice new sounds,
A new attitude was born from the smile and
frown,
Changing outfits like I wear this game like a
crown,

Create your own path don't copy and duplicate,
Don't believe everything your told and don't
prevaricate,
Learn your lessons and ameliorate,
Because it is all part of the game,

I must get rid of oppression and killing of the
innocent,
Non stop hustle no time to be indolent,
Walk in a room like the definition of confident,
No time to be diffident,

If I'm not the drug man,
If I'm not the crime man,
If I'm not the billion man,
And if I'm not her man,

Then I'm labelled as lethal,
So best believe I'm the man who will get
freedom for my people.

At 7 I knew I was going to be someone big, I knew I was going to be a big deal. I just didn't know what I'll be doing or how it will play out. To be honest I didn't care, I was too hungry to notice what plate I needed to eat from. I just wanted good food.

Few years later I realised waiting around for someone to cook me some food was hopeless. I have to do it on my own, so at 14 I decided to cook my own food. I don't know why but for some reason I've always been on a different level. My thinking, my attitude and my energy has always been different from everyone.

While most kids my age were thinking about what games to play next, I was forced to question why life was the way it is. Why did I grow up without my parents, why is there inequality, why is there racism, why was my father abusive towards my mother and why is there poverty?

The only people that showed me love and respect are the ones that were in gangs and lived most of their lives on the streets. When I was homeless my brothers were always there for me and everyone else betrayed me which I'll never forget. Even though I wasn't part of any gangs, I knew brothers from different ones. I was blessed with all of them and we understood the level of survival we had on our shoulders. Now most of them are in prison, maybe I would be too now but life had different plans for me. Since little I was always mad, that's why I always had fights and didn't take any nonsense from anyone. My elders saw that I got no fear, I speak less , listen, observe and do more. They didn't want that life for me and I knew I didn't either. I was just a kid looking for his freedom.

People need possibilities to think they got a chance, you can fail all the time but you only need to win once.

I'm failing all the time, even my wins right now. I don't count them as wins, yes I celebrate my wins but I don't define that to be the win that will tell me, I've done it. Everyone will have their own definitions of winning and what will tell them that they have done it. I know I have done it when I have completed my mission, helped enough people and be able to live a life full of adventure with my soul mate. Even if that does not happen, maybe it was never meant for me? Then I'll still be happy because I know I've enjoyed the process and the journey. Instead of waiting to reach the done it level and then be happy, I'm happy now and happy while getting to the done it level.

That is still a win for me. That is enough for me to be satisfied and content. If you want to know more about me, read my book Mitak's Incomplete.

I was always in rage, even though I seemed calm I was itching to get something done. Matter of fact even till this day I still have that rage, I just know how to control and handle it better. Everyone underestimated and doubted me. Told me I'll fail at everything, but guess what, those same people, are the ones reading this book now. Aha.

Most people talk like they know it all, truth is they don't. No one does. You have to find your own way, make your own way. Don't worry about what others got to say.

So you want to know about grinding and hustling huh. Okay, Let's see if your up for it.

01. Work ethic & Energy

You want success but are you ready to work for it? How bad do you want it? You have to master the work ethic, it is not just about working hard but working smart. It is about knowing what motivated you and what feelings to trust. I am sure you have heard people say, "I don't have the time" or "There is too much happening in my life so now it's not a good time". If you really wanted it, would you even say that? I get it, life might put you through some hard struggles that might stop you from doing what you want. I know all about that. But that is when you have to check where your priorities are. If you have time to sit and watch TV or Netflix, then it's just all excuses to me and it tells me you are not that serious. You talk about all these big goals but decide to do nothing about it? So are you just all talk then? It's great having all these ideas in your head, but nothing will happen if you don't get up and start executing. Sometime sacrifices have to be made in order for you to work on your craft. So tell those friends, not today because you are busy building an empire. Like the great Harvey Spectre says "The only time success comes before work is in the dictionary."

Before I left care, they put me in a semi-independent housing. Where I lived in a room, a small fridge, a small table, bed and a cupboard. I was unemployed at the time and only had about £40 for me to survive for the week. My mental state was a mess during that time and most of the time I felt like doing nothing. Just giving up with everything. Most nights I went to sleep starving and didn't have much to buy new clothes. Through all of that my energy never changed, in fact it just got stronger and stronger. I was hungry physically but more hungry spiritually and mentally. So I sat all night writing my first book and a whole blueprint to starting a business. I wrote plans and goals for me to achieve in the years to come. At that moment I pushed myself, I forced myself to work and think. Try this, get off your phone or get away from any distractions. Just sit there and do nothing, watch the world or take a look around wherever you are. And just think, let your mind explore, ask questions and think about what you want to. I didn't have much money to be on a phone contract like most of my friends, therefore I didn't have much mobile data to be on Instagram or watch YouTube. So I was hardly on my phone. I think that helped me more because I didn't have that distraction of constantly being on my phone. My motivation was on a different level at the time ,I was already at the lowest point life could put me in so it just made me want to fly higher.

Everyday I worked on my goals, step by step. I

had to discipline myself so much and the harsh conditions I was living in just made me feel sick and in so much rage that I just couldn't stop working. I told myself I need to keep working till I no longer need to see this anymore. The true principles or life, know what you want, don't let people walk over you and don't forget all the scars you try to hide. You always have a choice to make, you are in control and if things are not the way you want them? It is because you haven't made it the way you want them yet. If you want to see results, you first need to put in the work. Don't make excuses, stop trying to make yourself feel better and start doing things that will eventually make you feel better anyway. I wake up at 6 am sometime 4 am, work out, read a book and then start working.

No one is telling you to work so much that you don't have a chance to relax or spend time with family and loved ones. Someone came to me once and said "Mitak, I don't have time in a day to do what I enjoy and like when I'm too busy working". I replied, first of all your work should be something you enjoy. If it's not then you are just torturing yourself. And secondly you can always make time. I get all my work done everyday and I still make time for my friends and do other things. I love anime, right now I am watching One Piece. That anime has nearly 1000 episodes, I started last month and already I have watched over 700 episodes now. At the same time I signed deals, rebranding my business, held meetings with my team, networked, wrote 3 books including this one, created so much content, started a podcast with my good friend Jesse and Siraj, networked with CEO's, professionals and completed over 20 projects for our clients. I'm just getting started. Everyday I am doing so many tasks I can't even keep count. That being said it doesn't mean overload yourself with projects and tasks. Only do as much work as you can handle, and this is how much I can handle. Well now I can, before I couldn't. But pushing myself so much now that even doing so many tasks a day doesn't seem like much for me. I still feel like I could do more.

Every time I push myself further and see where my limit is, the more I realised there is no limit and I just keep going. Further and further. Yes work is important but that doesn't mean you forget about sleep and food. Right now the most important thing for me is getting enough sleep and eating a lot of food. I eat, sleep, pray and hustle like mad. Your work ethic has to be crazy, so crazy that it becomes like muscle memory. When you brush your teeth, you don't need to think how to do it each time. Likewise when you are working and hustling it's like second nature. I grind all the time and I hustle all the time. I got all these ideas flowing through my mind, that I don't know what to do with them. I have to write them down and keep them for later. It's all about timing, everything has a time to make it's entrance and to be introduced. Just like you, you have a moment in your life that will change everything for you. That will be your moment, your time. Just like I know my time is coming.

Sometimes you might feel like nothing is happening, but that is when you have to remember everything takes time. You just have to keep working and everything you put in, it will come back to you for sure. I use my struggles and suffering as fuel for my motivation, which then helps me have this unstoppable energy that helps me increase my work ethic. There have been many times I didn't want to leave the house. All these networking events, I didn't want to go. But I chose a nice suit to wear and decided to go anyway. I used to get thoughts like, don't worry, leave it, go another day. Then I told myself, no I can't stop now I have to keep going. I'm still not where I want to be so how can I relax like I am? Plus I got a lot of people to prove wrong. And I still got my island to buy. So why am I so ambitious and why am I doing all of this? That's easy, I want freedom. Freedom to live how I want, do what I want, to free my people and freedom to rule the truth. Most people will say they want to be rich and we know they will do anything to get there even if that is walking over others. That's not me, what I am trying to do is bigger than me and you. You have to believe in what you are doing, if you don't believe, then no one else will.

Consistency is the key, working on that goal. Break it down and start executing it. It is so easy nowadays to become millionaires, you can do one dumb thing and become famous or do something meaningful and change lives forever. The choice is yours. Take a look around you and see how much opportunities there are out there. 50 years ago if I wanted to talk to someone across the world I will have to write a letter and wait few days for a reply, now it just takes 2 minutes to send a message or connect through socials. If you want to talk to the decision maker at Apple or Nike, what's stopping you? Fear of rejection? come on now.

When I walk in a room, people feel my presence now and not only that after staying quiet for a while when I open my mouth I leave their mouth open in silence. Some feel jealousy towards me, some feel intimidated and some feel inspired. Either way I'm glad I can help you. Aha. Just remember, respect is not demanded it is earned. Through it all remember to stay humble.

Here is a piece of advice, talk less, listen more, observe, think 7 steps ahead, come up with ideas, create don't copy, showcase don't show off, don't have expectations, failure is like a sour sweet just eat it, rejections is like trying to catch air just let it go, don't care about what others are doing or saying, be selfless, be confident, be hungry, don't act like you know everything because you don't, keep learning, don't feel entitled you only deserve what you put in, create your own legacy, let them laugh, let them hate, let them doubt you because the sweetest revenge is self improvement and winning. The game is very simple, stand out, be different, solve problems and hustle with every breath.

02. Patience & Making the right moves

They say I walk around like I got nothing to lose,
Maybe I am a threat and a living proof,
An individual that doesn't fear death,
A limited time only offer that was too good to be true,

I can't play the middle man,
I am either calm or Psycho,
It's hard to play by the rules,
when things are not stable though,

I'm nice when I need to be,
I work hard like no ones watching me,
you can play me it's cool,
but at the end you'll just find out that I was playing along too,

I can't be bought or manipulated,
some people want you around because they see a benefit in you,
There is nothing stopping me and that will make me prosperous,
That is why they know me to be dangerous,

*Some will talk moves before doing anything,
they will talk big and want things instantly,
forgetting that the key to success is
working silently and patiently.*

This is a big one, and a very crucial element to winning the hustle. We live in a world today where everything is given to us almost instantly. I can order something on Amazon and can get it tomorrow. I don't feel like going out to eat tonight, order something online and get it delivered. You could say we are spoilt with so much ease and options. It has made some us very lazy. Which is a very bad trait to have if you want to be a good hustler. Although this had made life so much easy for us, it has also made us impatient and has caused our attention span to be very short. When you are waiting to go to a meeting are you on your phone? If a video does not interest you in the first 10 seconds you will skip to the next. Take TikTok for example, the infinite scroll effect is a brilliant feature to keep users on the app longer. You can spend 4 hours just scrolling through videos and it won't end. You will be shown videos after videos. This feature works so well that even Instagram has introduced something called Instagram reels, so has Snapchat. Why am I mentioning this? Well it is important that we don't allow this to make us impatient when it comes to the grind and hustle. When it comes to the hustle, it is a complete different mindset. You have to step out the normal mind frame you are in everyday and discipline yourself to think differently. Create a new mindset, a better mindset.

You have to be careful with what habits you have. The last thing you want is to be on the journey to success with a lot of bad habits, which will not only make you lost but damage your ability to carry on going when things get tough. And in business or when trying to achieve success trust me, it will get tough, very tough. I'm sure you have heard the saying "patience is the key". Well it is true, without patience a lot can happen to you. When things go wrong that is patience testing you. Will you give up or keep going? There was a time in my life where I was not getting the results that I wanted. Things was going completely wrong for me. I knew then that I had to be patient, I cannot expect myself to become a millionaire or a billionaire over night. Even though that was not my goal. I couldn't care less if I was rich or not. My success is determined on my level of freedom.

I realised that I was rushing a lot of the process. Anything from finding your passion to doing what you need to do, should take time. It is the process, that brings the hustle to life. I enjoy what I do, everyday I get out of bed and I can't wait to start hustling and working for my goals. If you are working to be happy or telling yourself that once I reach that goal I will be content and be happy? All you are doing there is torturing yourself. What about enjoying the moment you are in now? Enjoying the process that you are going through now? You see, most people go through life waiting to be happy once they have this or be in this position. But what they don't realise is that this is actually ruining their energy, attitude and hustle. It actually ruins the motivation levels and makes you perform badly. So let's be more patient and enjoy the process.

Now let me tell you about taking risks, the grind and making the right moves.

"In the morning he shall devour the prey, & in the evening he shall divide the spoils. If you don't devour when you are young? You'll have nothing to divide when you are old." - T.D Jakes

This really hit me, made me understand the true nature of the grind. What does it mean to really work for what I want? How do I know if I'm on the grind? I started thinking and looking back at every step I took. Everything I've done until this moment. What did I do? How did I spend my time? At first I was worried because what if the answer will be you didn't do enough. But I was wrong, I did do enough. I worked so hard, gave it my all. Everyday I would work on my dreams, wake up early in the morning or go sleep late at night. Reading books, watching videos, following successful people and even attending networking events to connect with people from all walks of life. Strangely enough, Somehow I feel like I didn't do enough, like I could of done way more. Really pushed myself to the limits and give it my all. Till I run out of breath or till I collapse into nothingness. Till my eyes became watery, red and sore. Till I could no longer stand up because of the fatigue. Until all the muscles in my body could no longer move, except for the muscle that puts a smile on my face. A huge smile from all the excitement and dopamine I get from grinding. That's how I wanted to work, like there is no tomorrow. Like I was short on time. That's exactly how I started to work and I soon begun to see the results right in front of my eyes. It was amazing! It's still is!

I rather work and suffer now then work and suffer when I'm old. When I have no more energy left and I'm no longer in my prime. That's when I should be relaxing and enjoy the remaining humble days.

I always felt like I'm constantly on the run, I had this weird uneasy feeling all the time. This feeling made me feel restless like I always needed to do something. Like I wasn't safe and secure. I was constantly fighting for my survival, I still am now. I can't stop, it's too soon. And at that point, for the first time in my life, I knew that this is what it means to live life on your own terms. To live a life full of risks and adventure, to be in control and most importantly to be free. At this point I knew that this is what it means to really grind. To really build something, from real blood, sweat and tears. To understand the meaning behind how powerful you can be when you put yourself to work. Want to know the best part to all this? Is that you really just proved to yourself that you can do something that you thought you never could do. You built something with your bare hands from nothing.

The days I was jobless and couldn't get a job was the biggest risk I took. The day I quit my part time job and said no this is not it for me, there is more to why I am here. I took the biggest risk. I put myself in a position where I had no choice, I had to grind and push myself. It was only then I unlocked my true potentials and understood the real reason why I was here. I had no income, no money coming in to help me survive. That was a test in itself, to really see what I'm made of. A lot of people want that 9-5 job because it's a sense of security but the bad thing about that? Is that you will never know who you truly are. What talents you have hidden inside you. All you will be doing is following someone's step by step to do a job. Make someone else rich and ruin your self worth. I stepped out of my comfort zone and decided to stop living comfortably. There is a reason why I want more, why I have all these dreams, so that means I have to go get what's mine.

If I said to you, whatever you speak into existence, have a sense of belief that is so strong and have faith, it will come true. Would you believe me? I used to think that was nonsense, until I started doing exactly that. But that being said does not mean you just believe and it will happen, you still have to play your part and put some actions into play. Just like a game if I created the most powerful player, it would not make me the most powerful player until I actually played the game and win.

*I told you I'm a soldier
Got no choice but to be a warrior,
Came out the dirt like I was inferior,
Then cleaned up like I was
superior,*

*This is how it is it's already been
written,
Way before I was born it had been
written,
I'm supposed to come here &
cause chaos,
This is my legacy you're living in.*

03. Always Learning

Don't make that mistake where you think you know everything. I know that may sound obvious but you will be surprised how many people forget that. Sometimes it is easy to lose track of what you know and how much you know. You may start talking like some expert which is fine, we are all experts in our respective fields. But once you have that know it all attitude, that is when it can become very dangerous and harmful to your development. You can never stop learning and you can never know it all. We are just humans, therefore we are not perfect, we make mistakes and we don't know everything.

There might be others out there that seem like they have all the answers, the good news is that no one has all the answers. Only the creator of this world and creator of us does. Regardless if you believe in God or not, I'm sure you can agree that we don't know everything. I think we need to sometimes humble ourselves and listen more. There is a reason why we have two ears and one mouth. We should listen more than we should talk. Instead of being so focused on trying to get our point across to the other person, we should stop, listen and understand.

When it comes down to learning we should apply the same principle only this time with some acceptance. Accepting that you don't know everything and everyday you need to learn something.

I have to go to the top,
because I've already been to the bottom,
and there is only up from here,
they get jealous of my empire and style I'm rocking,

Let me explain something to you,
I'm a old sage stuck in a young body,
you can out word me but I'll out work you,
I'm original while you just copy,

I'm a hustler and a living legend,
walk in like I don't care is my theme,
Don't talk to me about the game,
when your all about that get rich quick scheme,

if you are a soldier,
I'm the general your saluting,
If your the general then I'm the king,
if your the king then I'm the spirit
you won't see coming.

Learning something new everyday will not only help you develop yourself but let you unlock a area of the mind that you probably didn't think existed. That area is what I call the secret vault. Where not only do you store every information but able to take that information and formulate it into something else. You are able to combine and update existing information. You can only unlock this area when you make learning something new everyday into a habit. It will become like muscle memory, Your brain will realise this new change and rewire itself. It will create this space for you where there is new information coming in everyday. That information and knowledge is not just sitting there but it is being used. Thus you have created the most powerful asset.

Our focus should be to constantly develop ourselves and learn new things all the time. Knowledge is power right? Well that is true. Whatever area of expertise you are working on, learn more. Master that area and upgrade your skill set. For example if you are a marketer or want to be a marketer you must keep learning. Learn new ways of doing marketing, what are the current trends? How do you execute the best marketing campaigns for your clients? You have to constantly better yourself, which then will allow you to provide real value that no one can resist. So don't stop learning.

04. Jealousy, Rumours & Downfall

Being successful comes with some negatives that you have to be very careful with and ignore. There will be times where a lot of people will be jealous of what you have or with what you are doing. You are always going to have people that talk down on you, don't like the ideas you have or simply don't believe in what you are doing. They won't like you when you have nothing but when you start focusing on yourself and start doing good, they will try come back into your life. Now all of a sudden they like you and apparently they always supported and believed in you. Yes even that one person that you liked, she thought you was worthless and boring until they saw what you've got going on now. Okay maybe she wasn't that attracted to you or the "personality" sucked. But if she seems interested now all of a sudden then something doesn't seem right. Does it? Well not everyone is like that but I am telling you this from my perspective as a young man that comes from a poor background.

I had to deal with all sorts of people that want nothing but to see you fail. Now I get all these people trying to get back in my life, I just ignore because I no longer know them. You didn't want to help me make the food, what makes you think I'll allow you to have a seat at the table? You have to be very careful of these type of people and keep them out of your life as far as possible. Have nothing to do with them. I pray people get what they deserve, even if that is burning slowly in hell because that is what you deserve. Your choices, your actions and how you treated others got you to that place. So it makes sense to pray that you get exactly what you deserve and make sure you don't miss one single fraction of punishment. I mean you can't always be nice and sometimes you have to be nice to those who deserve your kindness.

Yes you should forgive and wish good on others, which I do to those that deserve it from me. However even if I did do that, it doesn't mean I have to see your face or have anything to do with you. I no longer know you or have anything to do with you. I mean why do people get jealous? Because they want something that you have and they can't have. Not realising that what you have they can never have and what they have you can never have. We all have our separate journeys therefore we all have separate destination and rewards. Maybe they can't do it for themselves so they get jealous seeing that you are able to do it. Or they are evil and just enjoy seeing others suffer. Either way, I think it is just dumb and stupid.

Because all of that effort and time you spend trying to ruin what someone else has, all of that planning and execution to make that happen. Imagine you used all that brain power onto something of your own? Put all of that energy into something you want to do and created something for yourself. Imagine how successful you will be. You might be more successful than the guy you was hating on and being jealous of in the first place.

There will be people who try spread rumours about you in hopes of ruining your reputation. They will try anything to see your downfall. Rumours and what people will say about you is unavoidable. People will always have something to say about you. But that is not the problem. The problem is how you react. Sometimes people will spread rumours about you just to get a reaction out of you. When you give them that reaction that is when you lose. But before that, you hold all the power and you can decide where the direction of that conversation goes. Yes you can clear up that rumour or accusation by simply saying, that is not true and is just a rumour. If you haven't heard it from my mouth then it is not true. Moving forward I will not be making any comments regarding this. That is all you have to say and just like that, the power of the conversation remains in your control. Your reputation remains strong and most importantly you just told people not to mess around with you. You know how to stand your ground. Now people will be careful on how they approach you, what they say to you, what they ask you and that you are not someone to be taken lightly.

I have so many people that have tried to ruin what I am building. They forget that one bad day at the office doesn't ruin my hustle for the rest of the year. I expect people to be jealous of me, It's part of the game. But when there is people from your own family that are jealous and want you to fail. That is some amazing stuff. Aha. Let me explain. Strangers will be strangers so to me it doesn't matter much what they have to say. But when family says some stuff that can kill your energy and feel like something is wrong with you. The truth is, there is nothing wrong with you. There is something wrong with them.

The funny thing is, I've had more people that are not family, support me and believe in what I am doing. They thought I won't be anything and always underestimated me. I don't speak much so to them that meant I am not a big deal, but little did they know. Where I come from we call them "snakes". They thought my kindness was me being too soft and weak. I am only kind to those who I want to be kind towards. Those not so lucky will have to deal with my ugly side. I realised soon that some of them get jealous when I speak about my future goals. Hence they will try bring you down because they don't want you to go ahead of them or do something better than them.

I cut of my relationship with most of my family members, like uncles, cousins grandma etc. Because they want nothing good for me so why should I keep them around to see my achievements. It's been few years since I saw them or spoken to them and life has been great. I am glad I got to see their true colours through all the fake love. Sometimes you just need to remove certain people from your life and move on. You just need to focus on yourself, surround yourself with people that uplift you and just do your thing.

So the reason why I said it is amazing? It is because I use all of that as part of my motivation, my fuel to carry on going. I've got a lot of people to prove wrong and the best part is that I won't need to say a word to them. All they can do is watch me. So let people be jealous and let them say what they want, It shouldn't matter to you. You should be on your grind and hustle regardless.

They don't want to see you win,
they want to see you fall,
they will smile face to face,
but really they want to cut you in half
when you stand tall,

I've always minded my own business &
tried to live as simple as I can,
but all they did is talk down trying to
make me feel like a less of a man,

You know they are jealous when they
start naming favours, just to make
themselves feel bigger than you acting
like saviours,

they don't care trust me,
they only care if your doing better than
them & making money,

They just couldn't let me chill,
You can call this hustle my last will,
All this energy just to destroy
someone real,
When they can put this energy in
building something to feel fulfilled,

Hating will only make you drown in
your own flood,
It's sad when most of your haters are
your own blood,

I know they've been jealous it's not
that hard to see,
Honesty & Loyalty means a lot to me,

It's cool they can pray for my downfall
& get jealous as much as they can,
I can't even stop my own destiny what
makes you think you can?

05. Kill self promotion & give back more

Toady we like to talk a lot about ourselves. I do this, I am like this, me and me. Yes we should talk about ourselves, but what we should be doing is be helping and giving back to those who need it. Ask yourself what do you do more, promote yourself or giving back. Your answer is closer than you think. The first book I wrote is talking about myself and about my journey. I wrote that so now it is out the way and I no longer need to explain my story. I can now focus on giving back and helping those that need me. Help my people.

We live in a world now where if you don't talk about yourself or promote yourself, you will lose. Where if you don't sell yourself properly you will lose, where if you don't explain your purpose or reason no one will support you. Where actions is not enough but if you talk big people believe you. If you sell dreams and make false promises you will have a my vote. Where the truth is right in front of your eyes and yet we will ignore it. Where if you are humble and modest it is seen as weak and those who flatter themselves you are seen like a hero.

I am more impressed when I hear someone talk

about others, helping others and what goals and visions they have that will help a lot of people. I do like to know people more about their story but if you keep going on about you, then I just lose interest. When it comes to business it is important that we focus on giving back.

When I say giving back, I don't mean just charity. I mean in all forms. Like giving back knowledge, experience, value and not keeping it all for yourself. If you want to be successful, give back value. If you want clients teach and give back. Take a look at some successful people out there, what are they doing that makes them successful. They must be doing something different that you are not doing. You will see that most of the time it is because of the value they bring to others. Let me give you an example, I do branding and marketing. What would you think is the best way for me to be successful? Let me tell you. At the start I was doing what most of you are probably doing right now, is going around and telling everyone what you do and how you can help them. Trying so hard to sell yourself, so every interaction you have with someone is hardcore selling. I soon begun to realise I was being selfish, I was giving off an impression that just says, the only person I care about is me so pay me. I soon realised that this is not the way. Then I started to just talk about branding and marketing. Talking about different topics on the two subjects that will help people. Delivering value, you almost have to become a teacher. When you really give back value and it helps people you will succeed for sure. And you shouldn't just do it so that you can succeed but be genuinely wanting to help people.

Think about how can you help people in a way that brings real value to people's lives. You want to create a space where everyone can learn, take something away from what you say and apply it to their everyday lives. Not just knowing about who you are and what business you run. So remember give back and stop promoting yourself so much that people don't understand your vision and goals. Build your reputation in a way people know you are the expert and that you are the one that can truly help them in their journey to success. We are all trying to succeed and make something of ourselves, so why don't we just help each other do that?

It's easy, it's too easy,
pitch, create and delivery,
grab attention
and start talking cheesy,
it's that easy,

right now you got all the tools
in your hand,
Stop with all the excuses
and go and claim this land.

06. True Leadership

So what makes a great leader? Some may think a leader is someone who gives orders to a group of people. Or someone that has high status and is very important. Yes, being a leader gives you a good status and importance but that is not what makes a great leader or even allows you to become one. A great leader is someone who is selfless, someone that cares about their people. You don't get to choose to be a leader, your people will chose you. If people are not willing to follow you, than you are no leader. You can chose to rule by love or fear but what is even better than that is ruling by helping those in need.

When it comes down to running your own company, most people put their customers or clients first then their employees. But in my perspective it should be the other way around. Yes your clients are important and a priority but if you put your team first and take of them, they will take care of your clients. Being a leader you have a huge responsibility to lead and set an example for others to follow.

A true leader will make sacrifices and always think of his or her people. A true leader is someone who is strong mentally and physically, confident, caring, kind, generous, forgiving, firm, strict only when required and is always wiling to go the extra mile. This means paying your people before yourself, feeding your people before you eat. If you have to eat the leftovers and stay a bit hungry, then do so. Just like a mother who chooses to feed her child before herself if there is not enough food left. A true sacrifice.

It is easy to just say you want to be a leader or think of yourself as one. But the question is, are you ready to be one? Respect is not demanded it is earned right? So is being a leader, you can't just go around and demand to be the leader, you have to earn it. What have you done for your people? What responsibilities have you accepted? Did you just make fake promises? Or are living up to what you stand by? Are you benefiting more or are your people benefiting more? Are you doing it just for show? Or do you truly care about your people? Are you willing to sacrifice everything and lose everything if need be? Are you able to make the right decisions? Are you able to say no to something that will bring harm to your people? Are you humble enough to let others take credit where it is due? Do you ask your people on what they think and take into account their ideas and opinions? Do you celebrate the achievements of others and let them know that without them none of this will be possible. Most importantly do you love and honour your people?

Sometimes we cannot do everything by ourselves, we need a team. It is important you start building your team. As a leader, you should be able to identify who will be just right and what role they will play. A good leader will know their teams strengths and weakness. You should know where to delegate work and how you can push your team forward. Most importantly listen to your team and keep them happy. If you are able to do that your team will take care of everything else. The goal should be to build an elite team, a squad that can handle any business. Be a leader that your team respects and create loyalty. Which brings me onto the next topic, building your own all star team.

*The hunger & struggle is always
there,
when poverty is the only thing you
can bear,*

*Watching the sun set on my sorrows
& despair,
I hustle so much I wonder
if I have enough knowledge to spare,*

*Living in poor conditions
do I have the right to complain,
the desires & temptations
that I betray,*

*Do I master this pain
& fight to live another day.*

*Every stutter & sound
tells me who is next,
next to get in my way
do I do something now or
wait for success,*

*Sometimes being alone can make the
hustle feel worth it,
Because you are building something
no one else can take part in,*

*She doesn't love you now
she won't love you again,
unless you have money & status
apparently that's the game,*

*This is the last of my worries
as I'm only focused on elevating
myself higher,
completing my mission & building
my empire.*

07. Build the all star team

There are some things in this world we cannot do by ourselves, no matter how much we think we are capable of doing something on our own. At some point down the line you will need a helping hand. I mean I wish we can do it on our own, it will be just you as the owner and founder of your company. How boring will that be right? I always say this to people when they ask about what I think makes a company successful, my answer is the same, it is the people and the team. But I am sure you know that.

I have been doing this since I was 14, wrote my first book and started hustling like there was no tomorrow for someone like me. I grew up in a way which changed my mindset completely. A way that I learned life was about survival, I grew up without my parents and without any guidance for the future that I needed to create for myself. So I raised myself and knew if I wanted something done I have to do it myself. This made me independent but also fearless because I soon realised I was taking risks and fighting for something that should be mine anyway. I learnt a lot of lessons quickly that some people take their whole life to figure out. This put me on a path to being the leader and the hustler I always wanted to be. The plan was, I establish myself first and then help others do the same. Although I knew the future depended on me, I am no fool, I knew you wouldn't be able to do everything yourself and at some point you will need a team to help you. You can tell a lot by how people treat you, and believe me I learnt a lot from how others treated me. Maybe it made me cold, wiser, smart, confident, fearless or just crazy. But whatever it is, I know it did me good. It made me know what I wanted and how I wanted to do things.

I started my own company at 19, Dijcom. At the time I was doing everything myself. Going to events, workshops, writing up my first business plan, networking and meeting different types of professionals like CEOs and important decision makers. I met people from different industries that helped me understand the structure of running a company and most importantly that 99% of businesses all work the same just different operation systems. Before this, I just learnt about business from my friends and mentors. Now I decided to start one and see where I end up. I had to go out there and experience it all. It was great, I fell in love with waking up early, wearing a nice suit, grabbing a coffee to go and start hustling. 5 am to 7 pm was the hustle motive that made me a beast. Pouring everything into building this business. I had to make sure that the business I come up with has to have a good structure in place, a good business model. I knew it couldn't just be about providing the best service or having the best product but what problems will I be solving and why would anyone care? I knew I wanted to build an awesome business which meant only one thing, to have the best team to make that happen. So a year later, Zak joined me. At the time, Zak was watching what I was doing. All these events I was going to wearing these nice suits and he wondered what I was doing. Me and Zak started talking and before you know it he wanted to be part of the vision I had for the world and for the world of business. I started taking Zak to networking events with me, he was really nervous so I taught him all I know. We even role played before we went to the events, how to talk to potential clients and business professionals. Soon he became so confident that he understood how to hustle like nothing is stopping him. I made sure that Zak worked as hard as me, even more and he does. Now every time I call him to see how business is going, he is always working and coming up with better ways to advance the company. After Zak, we grew the team even more and now we have a really strong team. This is just the start, I have no doubts that our team will grow even more and we will dominate the world. It is really important that others around you are on the same level as you and singing the same song as you. They talk about the same vision and even making it better. It is your responsibility to make sure the team you have around you are taken care of, happy and being unstoppable. I am happy with the team I managed to build and I am making sure they are constantly learning to better themselves and going above and beyond. The team I have now are loyal, believe in me, follow the vision and see me as their leader that will take them to new heights. That's my all star team.

You see that, that's your future,
I said where,
Trust me young brother she
don't care,
You can't be so silent
you have to be loud,
be someone your not, like white,
Haha good joke but I am
brown and proud,

Look just get a job,
don't think this will work out,
when you make it don't forget me
in other words don't be a sell out,
and that's how people
project their insecurities and doubts,
the worst thing you can do
is listen to that nonsense,

A diamond is still a diamond
under all that dirt,
I'll never forget the ones who
treated me like dirt,
when you leave this world

all you will have is dirt,
You won't get in my good books
no matter how much you flirt,

I don't need you I can
open my own doors,
That's why I am here working
so hard because I want more,

So sacrifices have to be made
and a strong discipline is the way,
work hard till everything is tailored made,
Damn right I'm a legend that's self made.

08. Master Negotiations & Sales

When it comes to negotiations and sales it is about understanding others. You might not realise but we negotiate everyday. Everyday we make different choices and we make decisions depending on what is good for us. When you was little you may have asked your parents for some chocolates every time you went shopping. They said no and you did your best to convince them to buy it. Then your mother said something like this "okay if I get you this will you clean up your room and finish your chores?" So you think about it for a bit and then counter offer with something like "I'll agree to that if I can have an hour on the game console as well." Your mother agrees and just like that you have learnt how to negotiate. Well the basics at least. Now I am sure you have probably read many books and watched many videos about sales or negotiations. So here is my take on it and hopefully it can help you.

A big mistake I see a lot of people make is that they go into a negotiation with the hopes of getting what they want. The example I gave at the start showed exactly that. You just wanted chocolates and your mother wanted the chores done. Both parties only had what they wanted in mind and it came into a conclusion of eventually agreeing on it. This technique works most of the time but in my personal opinion it is a rocky start to the relationship. As humans it is natural for thinking about what we want first before we think about anything or anyone else. It is natural to be a bit selfish and think about us before anything else.

However when it comes to negotiating we have to be the opposite, be selfless. We should be able to go into a meeting thinking about how we can help the other person and not ourselves. When you walk into that meeting everything has to change. Your body language, your behaviour, your language, listening and the way you communicate. If you have read the book, "How to win friends and influence people." by Dale Carnegie. There are two principles that I really like. The first one is to be genuinely interested in people. Let's say there is someone you would like to speak to or meet. They could be someone really important or someone that is a leading expert in your field of work. What would be the best way to reach this person and get their attention to have a conversation with you? Are you only reaching out to them because you have selfish motive and want something from them? Or are you reaching out to them because you are genuinely interested in them.

Check your intentions when reaching out to someone and be interested in what they are doing. Have interesting questions to ask them that they don't normally get asked. By doing this it will make you stand out because I am sure they get thousands of messages and mail everyday.

We all want to be respected and valued. We all want to be heard and listened to. This still applies to when it comes to negotiating. Imagine if we walked into a meeting acting like we know it all, you sit down like you know you are needed. You pay no attention to what the other person is saying, you just keep talking about how you are experienced and an expert. You've done all this cool things and worked with this many people. You don't give the other person a chance to talk much and at times you even interrupt them with what you think. By doing this you have made the other person feel like they are not so important and completely disrespected. They now feel like you don't really care about them. Maybe they had a problem that you could of solved and by them working with you will be the solution to that problem. The deal was there but because you did that now, chances are they would not want to work with you. So now you have walked out that meeting without knowing what problem this person was having with their business and if you could of helped them. Not only that but you have also ruined a good chance to have a strong relationship with this person. You could of had a great partnership that would of really helped you, all because you didn't pay enough attention and give the respect to the other person that they deserve. You chose to talk more instead of listening. You was listening to respond not to understand. There is a difference. You didn't let the other person know that they are important and you care enough to respect them and listen. People say more than they want, if you listen closely you can understand.

When walking into that meeting, walk in with less pride, less ego, be humble, passionate, logical, kind, respectful, determined, positive and be more understanding. Learn to connect, be social, confident and have fun. Find a common ground and create a space where you both can work together. Where you both benefit from this partnership and push each other further. Don't take anything personally and respect

each others perspective and opinions. Finally once all
of that is done, you can now sign the deal. Oh yes,
always leave on a good note. We meet people for a
reason always remember that, so even if they are not
the one right now it doesn't mean they can't be in the
future. Every human we meet on this earth has
something to teach us and something of value to us.
In negotiation we have to leave the conversation on a
good note, don't put a mark on the new relationship
before it has a chance to flourish. Because there may
come a day when you need to call in a favour and
this person can help you. Not only that, when you
leave things on a good note it goes to show what kind
of person you are. Regardless if they are able to help
you in times of need or not. It goes to show that you
value the relationship more and understand that life is
too short to make people unhappy with you when
there is no need for it.

Leaving things on a good note does not mean that
you have constantly speak to this person now or that
you have to become their friend. Unless if you want to
of course. But if you don't want to, then it's fine. You
can still have a good relationship with this person.
When you leave things on a good note, what you are
doing is leaving a positive impression and a good
memory of you. So the next time this person sees

you or speaks to you, the first thing they will think of is that good memory and impression you left on them. Be real, instead of trying to be something you are not. Be yourself and don't try so hard to impress. Most people can tell, your energy speaks thousands of words even if you don't at times. So remember, body language, what you say, how you say it, eye contact, being humble but classy and everything I have said in this chapter are key.

I got enemies that admire me,
friends that are loyal to me
& women that love me but can't be with
me,

Losing my train of thoughts,
I see the end coming like a speed train,
It's the don & vigilante within,
Am I joker or Bruce Wayne?

They want me gone
so they bury me with lies,
A kingdom without a ruler
and a empty throne that cries.

09. My philosophy for life

1. **Be humble and grateful for everything you have.**
Sometimes our ego and pride can get in the way of everything. It can cloud our judgement and decision making. We need to be more humble and appreciate all the blessings we currently have in our lives.

2. **Be patient and you will be rewarded.**
Don't rush anything, take your time. Let things play out. Life doesn't work on your schedule, it works on its own accord. So put your all in and be patient.

3. **Don't be selfish, instead be selfless.**
Give more then you take. It's not always about you. Think about others more often and live in a way that allows you to help people on a daily basis.

4. **Treat people kindly and take care of them.**
Treat others how you would want to be treated and take care of them. It's not just your family but you

should look out for anyone in need. Like helping someone old carry their shopping home. It is our responsibility to look after the planet we live on but also everyone who lives on this planet too.

5. **Love your parents and spend every moment with them.**

Parents are a precious gift to us. They teach us the way when we are too young and they give us comfort, support and wisdom as we grow older. So it is important we love them and take care of them when they get old. Not many of us are lucky enough to have parents but if you have yours, then love them and always be there for them. Always respect them and have patience. Don't lose your cool just like how they never lost their cool when you asked thousands of questions everyday when you was little.

6. **Live life the way you want.**

Don't ever feel like you are not in control of your life. That's not true, because you are. No one can tell you what to do, what to say or how to live. The choice is always up to you. No matter how much society tells you otherwise. No one has any power over you and they will never have any power over you. We all breathe the same air, no one is superior or inferior to anyone. It is your life and you only have one. So you get to decide what you want to do and how you want to live. Be happy and always make the right choice.

7. **Aim for freedom and make sacrifices.**

Sometimes in life we have to make sacrifices in order to be happy, heal and move on to the next chapter. Sometimes you have to sacrifice playing games or watching movie to focus working on your business. Even going out with friends because you have to stay in to finish off some paperwork. One way that can help you make the hard choices is thinking about your end goal, the big vision on where you want to be. So if going out is all you want to do in life and that is your big goal then go ahead and do that. However if it is not, and it is a goal like achieving total freedom like me, then going out wouldn't help that vision.

8. **Surround yourself with people that push you to do great things.**

I am sure you have heard that saying, your average salary is the group of people you hang out with. Or something like that. Well that also applies to everything in life not just your salary or income. It applies to how you think, how you behave and even your lifestyle. You need to find people that align with your visions and goals. People that inspire and motivate you to always do better. That think differently and that achieve greatness in a good way. And if you can't find anyone like that, which hardly happens given the current world we live in. Then start being that person you would of liked to surround yourself with. When you do that, then it will attract those types of people to you. Surrounding yourself with the right people doesn't mean just physically me knowing this person or being around them. Although that is a bonus. But it means, what is around you all the time and what is involved in your daily lives? It means what types of videos are you watching on YouTube or what types of accounts are you following on social media. What kind of books are you reading? What type of information are you taking in everyday? What sort of things are you learning everyday? And are you eating the right foods for a healthy development? This idea of being surrounded with people that push you to do great things, applies to all areas of life and mainly involves, what and who you have around you.

9. **Give charity and help those in need.**
Always give back. No matter how rich or poor you may be, always give back to those in need. Charity can be given in many forms, not just money. When you help someone and give back, that is called charity. When you feed a village, that is called charity. When you share wisdom, knowledge, experiences and educate the next

generation that is charity. When you move one with life to make the world we live in a better place, that is called charity. If you do have money, then I ask you please help the poor, the orphans, the ill and elderly. The people that need support, that need just one chance. Help them and life will reward you beyond comprehension.

10. Life is simple, it is us who make it complicated.

A lot of the time we misunderstand how simple life really is. We get so caught up in worldly desires that we don't realise that everything is temporary and one day we will leave here with nothing. What do you think the first man and women on earth worried about? For them life was really simple. When you get hungry, eat, when you get tired, sleep, when you want to travel, go explore. That's it! It was that simple. The earth was made for humans to enjoy and live a life we are all happy with. So what happened then? Why isn't it like that anymore? Well as the population grew and trust in humans to do the right thing became rare. Civilisations grew and so did crime. Greed, jealousy, power and envy became common. So what did we do to tackle this? We introduced rules which we called laws that made sure everyone had security and safety. We decided to create a system to have order in the world *otherwise there will be chaos. Then different civilisations and nations started trading. Trading materials and resources that were hard to find in the place they was living. Eventually money was invented and a new way of trading was introduced. Humans need to follow the law and contribute to society by working in exchange for money. Now food and other essentials were no longer free, you had to work for it and buy it using money. So what made everything so complicated? Is it, that humans can't be trusted to live in harmony and peace. Or is it that humans couldn't simple know when they have enough and share what was left? Isn't the earth big enough for all of us? Don't we have enough food to feed everyone? Does chasing after the world make us more depressed and unhappy? Imagine if food was free and land wasn't claimed by anyone which meant we could live anywhere we want and eat anything we want, when we want. You're probably thinking well it isn't that simple. Of course, you are right. It was just a thought, oh well worth a try. On to the next point...*

11. Laugh, eat, pray and smile.
Well, this one is pretty self explanatory.

12. Problems and stress are part of it, learn to deal with it.

From tomorrow you will no longer have any problems and stress. It won't exist. I am sorry to say that is not true. They are here to stay with us, through every moment of our lives and that is just how it is. You may think well other people seem like they don't have any problems, I mean look how happy they are. Truth is, everyone has problems and stress. It may seem like they don't because they have figured out a way to deal with it. So what do I mean when I say, learn how to deal with it. Let me explain in the best way I can. We will always have problems and stress, for example I know next week there will be a problem that will stress me out. So I am ready for it and when it does happen I will find the cause and then the solution. That way I don't waste time stressing out and worrying. Instead I accept that this is a problem so how can I solve this and move on as soon as possible. For me, just know that I will be faced with a problem soon helps me deal with it. It gives me a sense of calmness and makes the problem smaller then it is. Now I know we all have different ways and methods when it comes to dealing with problems. So what is your way of dealing with it?

13. **Acceptance is the first step to solving everything.**
Again this is also self explanatory and plays nicely with the previous point.

14. Everything is temporary, including why you are upset right now.

I always say... if won't matter in 5 years, don't spend more then 5 minutes being upset about it.

15. Don't get angry over small issues, let it go.

Is it really worth it being angry over this right now? Or have you got better things to be doing right now? Come on we have to get back to this hustle!

16. Stay 7 step ahead, 7 because it is my favourite number.

Did you know the world class chess players always think few steps ahead, most think 7 steps ahead. They are able to predict what moves you will make and even know the outcome before you do.

17. It's not always about you.

A lot of the time we think it is because of me, it is not.

18. Leave a legacy behind for people to remember.

Your legacy is the memories and the people you leave behind. It is the love and respect that people will have when they think of you, while you are alive and when you pass.

19. **Love more and hate less.**

Now wouldn't that be nice? Hmm...

20. **Work hard for the life you want.**

Even when times are hard and things may seem like they aren't going your way, you have to keep going. Even when you are faced with thousands of failures, which you will trust me. Keep working hard and working smart. If you are not happy with the life you are currently living, change it. Work until it is the life you want to live.

*When I wanted to help they asked who
I was,
When I came with solutions
they said we don't need your
expertise,
When I spoke of ideas they called me
a fool,
And when I shared my pain
they gave me no ease.*

10. When it all goes wrong

It will go wrong. Everything will go wrong and there is nothing you can do to stop it. Even when you think you prevented one thing from going wrong, something else will go wrong. It always does. That is just the way it is, you just have to accept it instead of trying to fight it. When it comes to the hustle you have to always remember this, because it will save you from a lot of things like expectations and disappointments.

When you are trying to get new clients for your business or trying a new marketing strategy, it has more of a chance to fail then to succeed. Even starting a business is a huge risk and could potentially fail. We go into business and the world of hustle knowing things could go wrong any moment. I have experienced this first hand. Even till this day things are always going wrong for me. In fact when I think about it now, it has never gone my way maybe just once or twice. But I guess that is all it takes to win, those once or twice moments where things don't go wrong. You can fail many times but you only need to win once.

When I finished school at 16 and started college studying business I also took on a sales job. This sales job was the hardest job I did at that time and really made me hardcore. It felt like I had gone through a military training in the world of business. I wake up at 4 am, exercise, shower, pray, eat and read before leaving for work at 5:30 am. I would arrive at the office at 6:30 am ready to start our team meeting at 7:00 am. After the team meeting finished at 9:00 am, we would have to go to a location in London and sell our products to local businesses in that area. We was tasked to sell a new broadband and telecommunication service for this new company.

We was out in the field from 9:00 am till 6:00 pm. At that point we headed back to the office to end the day with another meeting concluding on how we did on that day. I used to get home around 8:30 pm, where I had only little time to eat, maybe write a page for my book and then go to sleep. Next day, repeat everything all over again. This was a 100% commission job, which meant you only get paid for the sales you make.

I only took this job because I wanted to try something

different, to get an experience and maybe learn something.

During my first week, I got 0 sales. Everyday I would go out in the field and get rejections after rejections. I think I updated the pitch about 60 times and my approach. But no matter what improvements I made, I kept getting rejected. Things kept going wrong for me and that week I started questioning all my qualities, maybe I don't have the skills or maybe I am just not good enough. Maybe I am just bad at selling.

It wasn't that my method was wrong or what I was saying was wrong. I just forgot that not everyone needs what I am selling or is looking for what I am selling. It is a numbers game so majority of people will say no to you. What mistake most people make is that they give up after a few rejections and put themselves in the nothing goes right for me category.

Things will always go wrong that is just the way it is. Especially in business everything is up and down, 98% things are always going wrong. The solution is really simple, if you can't take the heat get out the kitchen. Aha.

From young, I have always been on my own. Most

lessons that life has taught me, I learnt after failing so many times. I have never had it easy, It's always been hard for me. I was 7 when I asked myself why things never work out for me, when I turned 14 everything that has happened felt like a fluke. Like I got lucky to have survived this long, at very young age I learnt that the hustle is like going into a ring with nothing and getting hit, not being allowed to fight back. You can only hit back when you have enough bruises to qualify to hit back.

Things never went the way I planned, I failed so many times. There was a long period where I couldn't get any clients for my business. No matter what I tried, I couldn't get clients. Even if I had the best marketing and lead generation system out there, everything kept going wrong for me. This wasn't a small issue like a filing error, this was a big problem because without clients the business can't grow or move forward. For a long time me and Zak struggled to find us clients and take the company to the next level. But for some reason it wasn't happening. The advice we got from others was everything that we have already tried so that didn't work either. This is was the perfect chance for us to say, "you know what, this isn't working out. Let's just close down the business." The thing is nothing in life goes as planned or how you want it to go and that it is true. Things will always go wrong, that's just how it is. We know this, but yet how many of us actually forget that. We go through life expecting things to go smoothly, we have so much hope and belief in our vision that sometimes it clouds us from the reality of, things will always go wrong.

What makes this all worse and doesn't help the situation is when you come across opportunities that show promise and it doesn't happen. When you come across people that only sell you dreams, use you and show you possibilities that were never there in the first place. You have to be careful with what people tell you, if you have discussed to work together make sure you have something in writing to make it official. If something is going good for you don't tell anyone, keep it to yourself. Although we want to share our accomplishments with others, most people don't want to celebrate with us. Don't tell people about your plans before you took actions and made it happen. And most importantly don't let people know what you are thinking. Because when you do tell them, you'll see why this thing that looked so promising didn't work out. You are sat there trying to figure out what went wrong? But you can't seem to find the reason why. Or maybe you do. Now I am not saying that everything that goes wrong is because you told people about it but majority of things that do go wrong is because although you had good intentions sharing your good news, others didn't. They seemed happy when you told them but deep down they wished bad on you, maybe out of jealousy or whatever reason they had.

The bottom line is, that a private life is the best life. Why do you need to tell people about your achievements? Will it make you feel better or is it their approval that you are looking for? You should let your actions speak for you, don't worry people will hear and see what you are doing. The news of your achievements will reach them anyway and catch them off by surprise. By then it'll be too late for them to wish bad on you as you have already accomplished your goals.

So I will ask you this question. When things go wrong, what will you do? And what process will you put in place to deal with it.

11. Time to retire

*Been through so much sometimes I feel
like I can teach what my ancestors
knew,
Been so broke all I could eat was 80p
noodles,
No rice or stew,*

*Been working so hard thought I saw my
missing poster on every lane,
disappeared for so long it's like they
deleted my character from the game,*

*I did this all on my own & made my own
way,
At this point I've become such a legend
I think I just need to retire & call it a day.*

Like 50 Cent said, "You're not making money until you're making money when you're not working." It's true, you need to be on auto pilot. You want to be on a beach relaxing while you're money doubles on it's own. You could be sleeping, dancing or using the bathroom and still getting paid. So you should be working on building a system that does exactly that. You want to have unlimited income and a lot of time till you start finding yourself getting bored. Then you start creating some crazy inventions out of boredom, that will make you more money or just give you a good laugh.

A lot of the time, I couldn't understand what life was putting me through. I remember one day I woke up and saw £16.71 in my account. Ever since I was little I always knew I was just a man on a mission. Most of the time, the mission wasn't that clear. I was facing everything blindly hypnotised by the beauty of the end goal, unaware of the obstacles that awaited me. So when I saw £16 in my account, I thought about what I will eat that day and what will happen to me on the days that follow? Will my ego and pride allow me to ask for help? Or will I sit here for a while and feel sorry for myself. Often I thought that my life will always be like this and maybe the cause of death for me is starvation. I thought about these things because for a long period of time, this is how I was living. Till this day I still don't know if this is my punishment or a beautiful curse that lies to me everyday.

I couldn't come home and say "Mum, what's for dinner I am starving." Instead, I was silent and my belly did the talking, rumbling in discomfort and pain. Looking back now, I managed to get through, somehow I always ended up eating. When I lost all hope, I somehow ate, it was like a miracle. Like a higher power was watching over me. My body was physically tired and hungry but in those moments my mind just shifted to a different gear. It went into a complete hustle mode. Like it separated itself from the pain it was feeling and only focused on the hustle. I know this wasn't that bad compared to when I was homeless, but this equally taught me an important lesson.

One night while my belly kept making noises, I sat on my bed just smiling and then laughing. Saying to myself "bring it, let's see what else you can throw at me. My only true enemy is me and at the time of vulnerability I will laugh at it with humility. I have nothing to lose, so what makes you think you can win, against someone who doesn't care what the outcome will be." It was then I realised, I am crazy and unbeatable.

At a young age, I learned very quickly that nothing beats freedom. I learned quickly how the world works and the people that live here. I learnt that most people are only here for themselves and in constant competition to out do the other person. I learnt that if you don't have money and status, you will get nothing. My only fault was that I was always kind to others and cared. But the world and the people of this world only treated me badly even if I was a innocent kid looking for his parents and a home. Now my kindness is limited and is not accessible to everyone. I stayed true to myself and didn't change for anyone even if the world is selfish, I'll still help and do my part.

As a kid I told myself that I want freedom and the only way to get it is being able get everything for free. Now how do I do that in a world where money talks. That's easy, making sure my money keeps on talking forever while I relax silently. Go from hustle mode to autopilot mode. I can't wait till I am 60 years old to retire because what's the point, I will be too old to do anything. That's no fun. I want to retire early while I still can dance carelessly with the waves surrounding my island. Aha! I just want a lazy life, where I can watch the sun rise to sun set and no one can say anything to me. I just want to chill, so let me chill.

For me it was like, let me do what I can right now before it's too late. I don't want to be old with no energy just thinking about all the things I could of done in my younger years. A life full of regrets as an old man. That's not what I want. Of course, most of the time I didn't even think I'll make it to an old age. I still don't. Who knows when my time will be up, it could next year, next month, tomorrow or even in the next hour. So why not live the time I have left doing what actually makes me feel fulfilled and gives me purpose.

While most of the people I knew followed the traditional route, finishing school, going to university, studying the typical subjects to become a lawyer or a doctor. Now I am not saying that this is wrong, I am just saying that this route wasn't for me. I don't know, but something just didn't click in me when I got told to follow this route. It was as if I wasn't built to process that way, I just couldn't do it. Even when I worked at a job, I couldn't function properly. I felt like my whole being just shut down and was restricted from achieving something great. I felt suffocated when working in that type of environment and my spirit was just fighting to get out of there. I realised that the more I kept heading down this path, the more I was destroying myself, trying to convince myself to fall in love with something that didn't cooperate with every fibre in my body.

Until the day I finally broke free and started doing what I was built to do. I started working on the things that actually felt good and made me want to wake up everyday feeling optimistic and motivated. I just couldn't wait to get started on my work and finally live the life I always wanted. From then on, I started to building a system, a system I mentioned earlier in this chapter. Switching on that autopilot mode and letting the hustle take over while you relax. Everything that you are doing right now has to set you up for the life you want to live, to retire from the world you can say. Now there is many ways to do this, I can list a few like owning real estate, passive income, dividends, equity and many more. The list is endless. But this is a journey you have to figure out for yourself, you have to find what works for you. You may even find or create a new way of income that has never existed before. Not everyone can own real estate and not everyone has the correct judgement and opportunities to get themselves the right equity that will set them up for life.

So what can you do then? What streams of income can you create and what types of assets will you choose? Do you want to run a business or just own one? It all depends on the path and choices you make. It all depends on the hustle and grind you put in now. What is the goal? And why do you want that? I know you might be thinking well, what about people like me Mitak, that come from poverty? How do we invest in things without any money? Believe me I know how you feel. I asked myself the very same question for years. I hated the fact that there are people out there with lots of money that can make things happen, it is so much easier for them. It's basically a head start to folks like us. Like imagine having £20,000 that you could use to invest into various things, like stocks that pay dividends or even a down payment to a property that can help you get onto the property ladder and into real estate. So what do you do then, if you don't have any money to start you off.

Well what I can tell you from my journey so far that you will have to take a longer route that won't be easy and will require a lot of patience from you. Now I am no way near to the success I want for myself, I don't think I am there yet so don't just take my word for it give it a go yourself. This path that you will take now will be filled with a lot of hurdles and challenges. It will require you to go the long way and although it may take you longer to get to where you want to be than other people, what matters is getting there, to your destination. Building your wealth from scratch with nothing is hard and very draining.

As we grow up, we are told to work hard, get good grades, graduate, get a job and then retire at the age of 60. And throughout the years people have been doing exactly that. I could never understand how a lot people were okay with something like that. You work your whole life to retire at an old age where you can't do much because you are old. But I guess some people might just say that's life. But is it really? Is that what you would call living? For me, I could never accept that and I never will. I have always had that mindset that I want to retire now while I am young. While I am able to do all the things I can, while I have the energy.

In life, you just have to know what you want and what kind of life you want to live. Are you living or surviving? It's not more money more problems, It's more money more freedom. They tell you that so you can remain poor.

So if you want to retire, you have to build correctly. Don't just focus on one stream of income but focus on building multiple streams of income. Everything you do should set you up for later. Your not just making money, you are building a diverse portfolio and an empire that leaves behind a legacy. Take small steps to achieve big results that pay off in the future. Even if you have little bit of money to start off with, put a small percentage towards assets that will double your income. Don't spend money on liabilities like fancy clothes and things you don't really need. Find what assets you can buy and keep building on that. Invest in things that put money in your pocket not the other way around. For example you are reading this book, this is a stream of income for me. Yes it took me time and effort to write this book for everyone to read, but now that this is published I can sit back and watch the sales go up. I could be sleeping and someone out there will buy this book and love it. I'll get paid while I am sleeping not doing anything. I am sure you get what I am saying now. That's just one example so imagine how many more ways there are out there that you can make money.

You will need to work constantly right now but the aim should be that eventually you can take a step back and push that autopilot button. You haven't retired until money is making money without you doing anything. So what are waiting for, start building towards retiring early and live the life you want.

12. Listen & Observe, be a good judge of character & learn how to read people.

Level 1: Listen & Observe
Level 2: Good judge of character
Level 3: Read people

Level 1:

A lot of people always ask me why I am so quiet. It's not that I don't have much to say, it's just that my mind is so loud my mouth doesn't get a chance to get a word out. Every time I walk in the room, I don't think about being the loudest in the room or the one with the most attention. I think about being able to go unnoticed and being mysterious until I chose to show myself. Until I know it is time to reveal my cards. Especially if I am in a room full of people I have never met or don't know that well. I even do this sometimes with people I do know. So why do I do that? Well it's simple really, I do this so I can read people and see what they are about. How do they behave and react to certain things? How do they speak and what type of language do they use in their sentences? What kind of personality do they have? Will I be able to hold a conversation with this person? Is this person someone I need to stay away from? Sometime it's good to just take a step back and observe others. This is about you learning about the character of a person before you even make contact with them. And when you do speak to them, let them do the talking. Just listen and ask questions about them. Find out what interests them and let them talk about it. Trust me, we love talking about the things that interests us. So much so that we end up saying, "Oh my apologies look at me rambling on and on about me, so what about you? I always say, the less enemies you have the better, most of the time we create our own enemies without even realising it. When you do what I just mentioned, you will have less people trying to win one over on you and more people liking who you are, what you do and most importantly they will enjoy having a conversation with you. This principle that I have is similar to, "How to win friends and influence people". When I read that book and applied that to my hustle and my everyday life, It completely changed the game for me. I unlocked so many opportunities for myself. I instantly became more likeable to people and oh yes you bet, more attractive to women. Aha.

Listening is so important, I think it is more important than speaking. A lot of the time I see people get themselves into debates and arguments that don't end well. Both parties are trying so hard to prove their point that all they are thinking about is their point and nothing else. I see this so meaningless because all you are doing is going in circles till the other person gives up. You may have proved your point but what did that achieve? Does the other person now like you even more? Do they now agree with your point? Maybe. But in most cases it just leaves the other person feeling embarrassed and unintelligent. We as humans love to feel important and smart, so when someone else says otherwise to us we straight away create this pull away negative emotion. That causes us to dislike the situation and the other person. Even if we know we are in the wrong. So what should you do then? Well before you get into a debate or argument, try to understand where this person is coming from. Listen to understand not to respond. Take in all the points they are are making and try to see it from their perspective. Ask questions like, "I am curious to know what lead you to this conclusion about this topic?" Sometimes it is the reason that's the problem not the opinion, so in order to change the opinion we may need to try change the reason first. Maybe something happened in you past or you had a bad experience with something that created this opinion. Deep down you know this opinion is wrong but there is something stopping you from getting past that. Maybe that is the reason, you need to revisit and look at it in a different view. If you had one bad experience with something maybe go back and try again to see if that can change your opinion. Or maybe you have to do more research on this topic because you didn't understand it properly.

After you have heard what this person had to say, then give your input and thoughts on it. Don't just jump in straight away and say, "you are wrong!" But instead say, "Look maybe I am wrong here and you are right but I think..." When you use those magic words, no one in this world will have a problem with that and most importantly this person now doesn't feel attacked. By doing this you have said that this is a equal playing field and anyone of us could be wrong, so let's not take it to heart. Even saying something like this, "Ok, I understand now why you feel like this and it does make sense. If I went through something like that maybe I will feel the same way as you. But let's say you didn't go through that or we looked at this in a different perspective, would you still feel the same way?"

Communication is so important in our world, not just when it comes to business or the hustle. And listening plays a huge part in that. When you just listen and observe, a whole new world opens up. You start to see how everyone and everything around you behaves and interacts with each other.

Level 2:

When it comes to the hustle, it is important for you to be a good judge of character. The last thing you want to do is get into a deal with someone that has no good intentions for you. Just like how you wouldn't want to marry the wrong person. You don't want to get into bed with the wrong person when it comes to business and building your wealth. Once you have mastered level 1, Level 2 is easy. Being a good judge of character will save you from a lot of problems down the line. It just makes you good at the hustle, it turns you into a magnet that attracts nothing but fortune and goodness. This is like the saying, "surround yourself with the right people." But this is on the next level to that. In this instance you are not just surrounding yourself with the right people but know which type of people and who you want around you. Most importantly who wants to be around you.

When I started my company at 19 I was trying to figure out how to charge my clients. I wanted to work with so many businesses and brands but I didn't know how to go about doing that. How can I provide my services in the best way I can to my clients and build a long term relationship with them? I wanted to work with some big brands but I knew that was too hasty. I started to notice that most of the clients we was getting were start ups that didn't have money. That became an issue because I wanted to get paid. That being said I still wanted to work with them and help them. So do I just do free work? No, not exactly. I came up with a solution for situations like this. Normally I would charge so and so amount on a retainer basis to my clients, if they don't have any money or can't pay then I ask them if there is a chance for them to offer us equity of their business. Giving us a percentage of the business or making us a shareholder. This allows us to still work with our clients and at the same time allow us to build a long lasting relationship. It's not just a one of project but a partnership that we both have to commit too. This also shows you are both serious and you are not just thinking short term and making money but thinking long term. Being committed to building something great and seeing the bigger picture.

Now I know you might be thinking, well no one will just give you shares of their company, if they just met you or if you haven't been working with each other for that long. How would they trust you? How would they know if you are good enough to be a long term partner?

Well the truth is, you never know do you? You don't really know someone's intention and what they will be like in the future. Unless you can read minds and see the future. You will never truly know. But that doesn't mean we shouldn't try. That is why being a good judge of character is key in this instance. Life is all about taking risks, I am sure you have heard that many times. Well it's true, if you don't take risks, you will always be stuck in one place and you will never be able to move forward. When you can be a good judge of character you will know if you can trust this person, will this partnership be beneficial and will this person be of value to what we are trying to build here. It's very rare for me to ask a business owner if I can be a shareholder in their company if I don't see potential in the business itself. I don't just judge the characteristics of the people I work with but also the environment, the people they have in the business and then the business it self. If the trust and all these other things is still stopping you, remember you can always get everything in writing. When I make a deal with a start up that is offering me equity in exchange for my services, I always make sure I get everything in writing. What am I getting from this partnership and how secure is this deal for me. Is my back covered in case something happens?

To be a good judge of character you have to see how

this person behaves around other people not just around you. Does this person keep their word and promises? Do they treat others well? Do they speak bad about someone when they are not there? Are they honest when it comes to owning up to a mistake they have made? Are they reliable? Do they have a similar energy to you? Are they as hungry and motivated as you? Do they know when it is time to take a step back and let others handle the problem? Do they talk big and take no action? Do they see your value and importance? Are they on the same mission or just passing by? Is this person really serious or just passing time? Do you share similar values and morals? These are just few things to consider, once you start practising these you will become a master. You will soon be doing this without even realising it because it becomes like muscle memory. Once you become a good judge of character it will improve your life hugely, in business and in your personal life.

When you are good judge of character, you will be able to know who you can trust, who is of value to you and if this person will become a great partner in the future or stab you in the back. This plays a big part when you are negotiating, networking, meeting new people and people that you already know. You will also be able to tell if something is too good to be true or if its actually genuine.

Level 3:

Reading people becomes easy when you master the first two levels. At this level, you will be able to recognise different personalities and characteristics that help you understand people. At this stage, you will be able to walk in a room and recognise what is going on and be able to read the room.

As a child I was always kind of loud and always happy to have conversations with anyone. More like a extrovert. As time progressed and as I started facing a lot of problems, I changed. The more pain I went through in my life, the more my mind became heavy and I became silent. The childhood I had was not the best and the way I got treated by people, I realised that no matter how innocent and nice I may be there will always be someone out there to take advantage of that. I made a lot of mistakes in the past just talking all the time, so if you speak a lot just be careful. Giving too much away by talking too much can put you into a lot of trouble right now or in the future. There are some people out there that will use what you have said in past against you.

Don't give them the tools to destroy yourself.

This goes back to the first level to just listen and observe, when you do that you are giving yourself the opportunity to read others. Don't reveal all your cards at once, play the right one at the right time. Don't let them know what you are thinking. Keep your opinions and your next move to yourself. Sometimes people might be in a bad mood and take out their anger on you just because you happen to be there. That's not because they are angry at you, but maybe something happened before they saw you that caused them to act in this manner. Now let's say they said something to you because they are angry about something else, instead of just listening and trying to understand the situation, you responded to that with the same hostility. How bad would that be? Really bad because now you are both angry. When you become good at reading others, handling this type of situation will be no problem to you. Sometimes all it takes is for you to say, "I can see you are not in a good mood today, is everything okay? Anything I can do to help? We can do this meeting another time if you'd like? After you say this, this personal will automatically feel at ease and most likely say, "yes, it's because of so and so.." or they might say, "you know what it doesn't matter, I am okay. Thank you for asking." They will now forget about what they was mad about and give you their undivided attention. By doing this, you just helped them remove what was bothering them and helped them clear their mind to get back to the current moment.

Being able to read others doesn't just help you but also help others around you. That's why it is so important in business and in everyday life. So remember these three levels as it will help you massively. They will make the ideal player in this complicated game and grant you wins in areas you thought you could never win.

I told you I can hustle it,
crush the diamonds & wear it as
armour,
sometimes I glitch from all the trauma,
You're either a goat or a llama,

I told them I am okay
but they didn't believe it,
Whatever you throw at me I'll
be ready to receive it,

They only offer help after you have
drowned,
but not when your flapping about
making sounds,

I told you I can hustle it,
but you didn't see it,
I am the king of the seas,
only I am here to swin in it,

I am a legend that just wants to eat,
It's easy to sin but hard to get good
deeds,
I am humble with no greed,
but I still need to let them know I am the

one they need,

I am a leader not a follower,
Trying not to be a slave & a borrower,
Credit, oh yes, Kaachinngg!!
that means you're slowly stripping,

Listen, don't listen to me,
I am just a lost kid,
Looking for a reflection through a window
that doesn't exist,

Keep you sweets in a box & lock it,
When they ask for it
say another kid took it,
When they find it empty,
say, hey! who ate it?

I just want to be paid what I am owe,
but they'll never give it,
because I have the ingredients to
make any plants grow,

All I can do is self destruct while I write,
because legends never die.

13. Legends never die

Being a legend is not easy. Like all the great legends that have come and gone from our world, they all left behind a legacy. That is what you have to do, leave a legacy behind. Something that people can follow and remember them by. Someone that motivates you, inspires you to do better in life. Someone that you consider more than a role model. Forget about being the wealthiest or the richest and think about, how you can leave your mark before you leave this place. You need to ask yourself, are you doing this for yourself or for the people you will leave behind. Leaving something behind for your family is important but leaving something behind for everyone is even more powerful.

When I wrote my first book at 13 years of age, I didn't even think of making it into a book. I was just writing about my life and things I was going through at the time. It was only later on that I decided to make it a book. And not only that but I decided to write the book in a way that it shows people how I have changed over the years and allows the reader to follow the stages I had to go through. I then realised that this book can actually help people even when I am no longer here in this world. That is when I decided to finally publish the book, because I knew this could change someone's life in the future. Even now this book I am writing, it will help someone out one day. I don't know if my books will ever go worldwide, maybe it will happen while I am still alive or it might happen when I am gone. I know the businesses I have and will build in the future and the people I inspire around the world will be part of my legacy. If you want people to remember you after you are gone, give them something worth remembering.

I have achieved a lot at such a young age and I know this is just the start for me and If I ever reach my ultimate goal which is to buy my own island and build a city. I know I have achieved something great and that will be a cool chapter in the history books of legends. Wouldn't you agree? I know once I have reached that, not only have I set my family up for life but also everyone else in the world. The books and stories that I will write will spread knowledge and enjoyment around the world. The businesses that I will launch will create many jobs and allow people to achieve financial freedom. Finally the city that I will build will house many people and also open doors of opportunities that can tackle poverty, world hunger and increase the living standards. Now you may or may not have such an ambitious goal like me but that doesn't mean you cannot be a legend.

When it comes to hustle, you have to think like a chess player. Recognise the pieces in your life, understand the role of each piece and how to play them. Most importantly, when to play them. It's all about the timing. Don't reveal your moves too soon or you will pay for the consequences. Even if you know this next move will make you win, hold off a bit and keep that move to the very end until you are certain of the victory. Don't let others know what you are thinking and don't let them know what you know. Don't get too comfortable, you have to be uncomfortable, the hustle has to feel like a burden to you. Otherwise you end up playing the moves too safe and when that happens you let your guard down. In chess the king is the most important piece but to me the queen is the most powerful piece. She can move anywhere and take out anyone. I always make sure to protect the queen first because if she is protected then the king will be safe too. That is why it is so important to play the queen at the right time, if you get too excited and play the queen recklessly then you lose your most powerful piece on the board, and your king is vulnerable. Take your time and think about the moves before you make them. Be patient and wait for the right moment.

Have a plan and a strategy, a step by step guide to get to your goal. Without a game plan and a strong sense of belief, it is going to be difficult to achieve your goals.

Being a legend you have to be able to get up, after all the rejections and failures, you have to get up. After all the struggles and sufferings, you still have to smile and welcome the change. The change that needs to happen within yourself before anywhere else. After all the pain and nights you stayed awake thinking, what am I doing here? Do I have it in me? Am I enough? You have to still wake up the next day and keep moving forward. You are not average, let me say that again, you are not average. You are much more than that, so why settle for anything less? You are a warrior, a champion and a legend. You are, your biggest enemy and you get to decide if you want to be the hero or the villain. You have to live with all the decisions and choices you make, so take responsibility and stop putting blame on others or yourself. You have to be willing to sleep in the mud before you can sleep in the penthouse. You have to accept your weaknesses and accept when you are wrong. You have to know what you want and go for it all the way. There is no option to quit even if you fail and there is no hope left. There is no such thing as giving up, only getter better every single time.

You have the key to your kingdom and your throne awaits. Be the legend we all know you are and we all know you can be. Even when you are gone make sure these lands and the seven seas echo your name throughout history.

The legacy you will leave behind tomorrow, starts today. Legends never die, that's what I always say.

Have I already gone past the point and there is no going back? Is this the path I've always been destined for? Am I that one that comes every 100 years to turn the world upside down? Have I already become too unnoticeable & dangerous? After all, I am now a man that has a purpose that cannot be touched, a sense of reality that can't be seen, a creation that only fears it's creator, a presence that cannot be heard, a energy that cannot be understood & a energy that cannot be tasted without the right ingredients.

Will I end up as the villain or hero? Will I exist as an untouchable knowledge or will I remain a secret. Hidden because maybe I came too early or too late.

I don't know if I'll lose in the end or if I'll be king. I don't know if I'll start a revolution that will live long after I'm gone. I don't know if I'll have my own army to defend the values I've set. I don't know if I'll be the one responsible for starting movements that will bring a new era. I don't know if people will follow. I don't know if I'll watch the world burn or watch it flourish. I don't know if I'll be able to buy my island and build my city. I don't know if I can be the leader they want me to be. I don't know if children will name me as their role model & say "I want to be like Mitak."

Mitak, what a strange name. I wonder if they will remember it.

All I know is no matter what I'll be a legend, alive or dead.

Now that you made it to the end of this book, I want to congratulate you and thank you. Thank you for taking the time to read this book and congratulations for making it this far. This was a test of commitment and if you're reading this then you have passed. This goes to show, that you do have it in you. You are interested in knowing more about the hustle, so you stayed dedicated and committed to finishing this book to the very end. This tells me you are serious and you have already taken the first step to hustling your way to success. If you are reading this for enjoyment or to learn about my take on hustle, either way I want to thank you. And I hope I was able to help you.

So the last thing I want to say is, remember, this is your life. If you are not happy with the way things are, you have the power to change it. Learn all the skills and knowledge you can and become a better version of yourself. Find what you are good at and master that skill. Start working towards the life you want now, not some day in the future.

I was breathing to get my life back on track when I had nothing and the only way I could do that was to hustle for the life I want. At one point I thought I'll stop breathing and that will be the end for me but I kept going. I told myself, as long as I am breathing I will keep hustling. So that is why this book is called...

Breathing To Hustle.

Breathing to Hustle (Part 2)

Let's be real you don't like me,
You only want my attention,
You want a 6 figure man,
But still work for your pension,

I told you I run things but
You thought I was just spitting game,
Everyday I'm a new man
So you'll never know me because I'm
never the same,

Look I don't choose to ignore you,
I just don't have the time to play
nursery rhymes with you,
I don't chase I attract so I don't love the
hustle the hustle fell in love with me,
I thought you knew,

I starved so much until I didn't want to
eat anymore, night or day,

*Your problems are like marshmallows
around the campfire,
the more you talk the more it will burn
& melt away,*

*I'm the type of alpha that make
Sure the pack is fed,
Sharpen my claws & when I've
spoken
They remember what has been said,*

*I'm like the treasure that has never
been found,
the light that reflects of the moon,
the gold under the dirt,
that is your doom,*

*Your love is like water that floats,
mine is like the sun
it never gets old,
you say I'm like the fire that doesn't do
what it's told,
your stare is like paper
it can make any man fold,*

I'm the king that sits with a empty throne
beside him,
waiting for the day when his queen can
be with him,
stay real close never leave him
I don't know if your words are deeds or a
sin,

Every time you get close to me your skin
burns
so let me extinguish it with your tears,
Let me drown in your love
until my flames become yours without
any fears,

Your like the hope that never dies
and the comfort that never lies,
the touch that never tries
and the presence that never testifies,

Maybe we are cursed to be so close
but never as one,
until we fight the world

and the mission is done,

I can finally have another chance
at holding your hand,
and disappear somewhere
we cannot be found,

It is this road that leads to you,
these signs & obstacles I have to get
through,
Your enough for me and
I'll walk as long as it takes to get to
you,

It is for you I did this all,
I search for you from winter to fall,
As the world spins
your love is the only thing that is still,
For you to be mine is my will,

Until then I will build our future
and build some muscle,

*so when the time comes I can swipe you
off your feet
and tell you all about how I was
Breathing to Hustle.*